ABANDONED COASTAL DEFENSES OF ALABAMA

THOMAS KENNING

AMERICA THROUGH TIME

To all the kids still playing fort.

America Through Time is an imprint of Sutton Publishing Inc
www.through-time.com
office@through-time.com

First published 2021
Reprinted 2025

ISBN 978-1-63499-283-1

Typeset in Trade Gothic 10pt on 15pt
Printed and bound in England

CONTENTS

ABOUT THE AUTHOR

THOMAS KENNING is an author, educator, and adventurer. He holds an MA in history from American University in Washington, DC, and teaches the subject in St. Petersburg, Florida. When he is not travelling to some far-flung corner of the Earth, he resides with his wife and daughter, planning his next improbable deed and trying to leave the planet a little bit nicer than he found it.

INTRODUCTION

I am not your typical military enthusiast. Yet here I am, writing my second book about abandoned forts. For me, the main draw is the "abandoned" part.

The thing I find most fascinating about these colossal structures—once regarded as so vital to the defense of the homeland—is that they are now relics. In their day, Forts Morgan and Gaines were among the most formidable weapons systems conceived by man, and now they are museum pieces, disused and crumbling under their own weight.

Alabama's historic coastal defenses were undone by still more advanced weapons: shells fired with fearsome power from the rifled barrels of steel artillery pieces, and steam-powered monitors capable of bellowing past before the gun crews stationed on the barbette tier could launch a second fusillade—the kind of nightmare combat made possible by modern engineering.

So, sure—in the short term, the cure may have been worse than the disease. But I still draw hope from this simple fact: The same human ingenuity that erected these brick behemoths also devised their obsolescence. If we can imagine such improbably horrible remedies for our species' woes, I think there's a good chance that we are also capable of inventing solutions that are just as proportionately humane.

It should go without saying that I am grateful to anyone who has served this nation in uniform– but I'll write it down anyway just to make sure that it is clearly understood. Americans are in their debt. We have a responsibility to pay forward their legacy of selfless service to their fellow man.

But it has long been my belief that our definition of national defense is too narrow. When it comes to the threats facing our country, too many of us are mentally stuck in the nineteenth century, when these antiquated forts were considered state-of-the-art. What if we more readily acknowledged the violence inherent in poverty, hunger, and animus, and added to that list the climate disasters fueled by our own worst excesses in the realm of irresponsible consumption and environmental destruction? What if we called these what they are—threats against our collective security?

How secure would a nation be that was using its wealth and expertise to lead the world toward the eradication of those scourges? How many of the world's other states would align in common cause, in the mutual defense, with that nation? How free would the people of such a nation be—from fear, from want—free to live their best lives in harmony?

Such a world wouldn't be realized overnight, of course. There is too much painful inertia to overcome. But the men who built these unlikely castles in the sand didn't achieve their ends with the easy snap of a finger either.

A great president of twentieth century said, about a literal moonshot of an idea, that the people of the United States accept the worthiest of challenges "not because they are easy, but because they are hard, because that goal will serve to organize and measure the best of our energies and skills, because that challenge is one that we are willing to accept, one we are unwilling to postpone, and one which we intend to win."

With that sentiment, I think Joseph Totten, master of Third System coastal defenses, would agree.

We are at our best as a people when, rather than resting on our laurels, we fix our eyes on the horizon and ask, "What next?" Though I've spent a good portion of my career writing and teaching about conflict, it is always from the supposition that violence, while occasionally inescapable, is anything but cool. Every dollar spent on a weapon of war, no matter how righteous the cause, is a dollar unspent on social justice, education, the environment, or any number of other worthy causes.

In that spirit—may all forts be abandoned!

Thomas Kenning
September 2020

1

THE INVINCIBLE

The sun rises on the Gulf Coast of Alabama, just like it always has. It's one of the few constants in these parts.

This beach has seen many would-be sovereigns come and go over the years. As early as 600 CE, indigenous people from the Mississippian culture constructed a substantial canal across the Mobile Point peninsula to accommodate both trade and transit—a sort of scaled precursor to the twentieth century's Intracoastal Waterway. There were later groups, too, like the chiefdom led by Tuscaloosa in the sixteenth century, who built mighty walled cities along the banks of the rivers that feed Mobile Bay.

France, Spain, and Britain built up early European colonies, ports, and stockades, sparring with each other for claim to these already well-occupied lands. Later came the United States, the Confederate States, and the United States again, whose combined armed and naval forces regained these shores in the largest single military action this corner of the state has ever seen.

But can any of these peoples—even now—lay more than a tentative, fleeting claim to nature's shifting sands? What will words like "Alabama" and "United States" mean to our descendants 1,000 years hence?

If the world is but a stage, then this rotating cast of nations has played a series of walk-on roles in Alabama's long history. They have each tried—at great effort and expense, with fortifications built on foundations of sand—to solidify their momentary hold on these shores, to extend their limited run by building a better stage of brick and mortar.

But the indifferent Earth is the true star, spotlit by the sun.

People speak of keeping two feet on the ground, like it's a firm, predictable place to be—but that's just as often *not* the case near the beach. The waves and the wind redraw the shoreline, sometimes too slowly for anybody to notice, one drifting grain of sand after another. Other times, like during a surging storm, the sea and the coast become one, changing faster than we can believe—revealing our human drama as the petty trifle it always was.

It seems someone has collected and arranged driftwood on this beach, perhaps with half a mind to start a fire. With the sun so low in the sky, Alabama in winter can get chilly. That's the mundane explanation for this teepee.

But it doesn't take much imagination—you don't have to squint too hard at this timber Rorschach test—to see a kind of child's play fort. Anyway, it's not so different from the forts I built when I was young—in the woods near my house, under a card table, wherever and whenever I could. If you've picked up this book, there's a good chance that you can relate—that you played fort, too.

What is it about forts that make them so appealing? Even as children, our imaginations are captivated by notions of shrewd defense in depth, protection from the cruelty of the world behind layers of dexterously laid brick and mortar. We relish the sense of security represented by a supposedly impregnable fortress, cleverly built to withstand every contingency—embodying the ultimate hybrid of cunning, ingenuity, and plain brute strength.

Is the love of forts a trait general to humans everywhere, a holdover from our earliest days on Earth as tiny, defenseless humans, as swaddled infants? Forts are like a security blanket or a mother's hug—warm, inviting, a pillar of support for all we hold dear. Firm and unyielding, like the harsh world outside—but on our side, standing tall and proud against anyone who would do us harm. A psychic balm, a panacea for all threats, real, imagined, or heretofore unknown.

Is the passion for forts more fervent in the United States than in other parts of the world? In the modern day, the U.S. accounts for approximately 40% of global military spending. We have divided the world into strategic commands and evaluate

Fort Morgan fishing beach on a crisp morning in early January.

our military might based on the assumption that at any minute we might need to fight two Iraq-sized wars with equal fervor. The story of a fortress for freedom, under siege by forces hostile to our way of life, runs deep in our national identity. It's a story told right there in our national anthem, recited like a liturgy of faith before every sporting event in the land.

The plan of a fort tells a story. Carefully considered defenses are like a strategy written in stone. These contingencies form a narrative upon which anyone can imprint their own way of life—a covert way there, a counterscarp here, a secure bastion there, all offering hope that our side will either turn the tide or fight to the last in a quixotic blaze of glory. From inside the walls, from atop the parapet, we can each plant our own flag, righteous and defiant, unyielding even when outnumbered and outgunned by a foe demanding our submission. Our ultimate perseverance is a manifest truth—with God on our side, in the form of geometry and physics—how can we lose?

I mean, as long as the waves don't rise too high and this concrete, laid on a drifting dune, doesn't crack beneath our feet …

Looking out over the east bastion of Fort Gaines on Dauphin Island toward Mobile Point and Fort Morgan, the modern visitor can see what all the fuss was about—the three mile-wide pass linking Mobile Bay to the north and the Gulf of Mexico to the south.

The terreplein is a flat masonry walkway behind the firing positions on the upper level of a fort. At Fort Morgan, between bombardment from Civil War artillery and decades of sun, sea salt, and temperature extremes, it is easy to understand why its edges have begun to fray.

2

A BRIEF AND SOMEWHAT ABRIDGED HISTORY OF COASTAL WARFARE AT MOBILE BAY

The beach north of Fort Morgan faces Mobile Bay. Aside from drilling platforms for natural gas—which didn't appear until the state authorized them in 1980s—this scene looks much the same as it would have through the fort's active years.

Alabama's coastline is not long—a mere sixty miles, comprised mostly of barrier islands, shoals, and the type of shallow, sandy shelf that tapers without hurry into the Gulf. The only natural harbor of any size or depth is Mobile Bay, an estuary fed by rivers which are also navigable far to the north, linking the interior of the state to the rest of the world.

Whether you arrived in Alabama as an eager merchant or a hostile invader; whether you imported enslaved men and women or exported cotton, timber, or coal (the ill-gotten products of their labor); whether you were mounting a blockade or running one, your business ran through Mobile Bay—the only direct route in or out of the state by sea. As such, this narrow channel connecting Mobile Bay to the Gulf of Mexico has played an outsized role in the history and economy of the Yellowhammer State.

Early European explorers were quick to recognize the potential of this site, even if it took them a few tries to get the formula for settling it just right.

In 1699, Pierre Le Moyne, sieur d'Iberville was charged with establishing a French presence on the Gulf Coast—an effort to compete with nearby Spanish and British claims. While surveying Mobile Bay, he discovered a traditional burial mound belching forth its grisly contents onto the sands of today's Dauphin Island. Interpreting this as the hasty disposal of evidence after some great act of violence on behalf of the region's "savage" inhabitants, D'Iberville labeled the small barrier island with a foreboding misnomer—*Île du Massacre*, or Massacre Island. In reality, this seemingly macabre scene was probably the result of the region's energetic coastal erosion, accelerated by the landfall of a recent hurricane. In other words, the violence D'Iberville perceived was not inflicted by man, but by nature, a product of the literal shifting sands of time.

The whole episode says a lot about the mindset of newcomers like D'Iberville, who were locked in a high stakes and often extremely violent game of continental conquest, fueled by their recent successes in navigating the open ocean. The French had the means to close vast distances in relatively brief periods of time—with the winds and currents in their favor, they could cross the Atlantic Ocean in less than a month. But they lacked the perspective or patience to fully understand the natural processes at work in the new lands which they scrambled to settle.

Case in point: in his haste to stake a claim, D'Iberville founded an almost completely undefended port on Massacre Island. This serviced a more thorough settlement further up the Mobile River, at the head of silty Mobile Bay, accessible only by boats of a shallow draught. La Mobile, defended by Fort Louis de La Louisiane, a chronically rotting wooden structure, became the capital of Louisiana in the years before the French could exercise a credible claim to the Mississippi, when New Orleans was a mere glimmer in King Louis's eye.

It seems almost inevitable that this tentative claim to the bay would slip from France's grasp. In 1710, Port Dauphin was seized by a lone English privateer. Simultaneously, La Mobile, now isolated from the broader European world by the sudden loss of its port, revealed its true nature—flood prone to a disastrous degree. The settlement was swept away in a flash, giving new meaning to the name "Water Street." Soldiers and settlers found refuge in the treetops, their timber walls and small arms proving little match for the rising waters of Mobile River during the rainy season. The site was abandoned shortly thereafter in favor of the city we know today as Mobile.

Fort Gaines sits a few dozen feet from the eastern edge of Dauphin Island. A stone seawall holds the line against erosion—a process driven primarily by currents, wave action in the channel, and the occasional tropical storm surge. The wall will do little to protect the fort from a rising sea.

To defend the rebooted colony, the French began construction of Fort Condé in 1723. Fabricated from sturdy brick and stone, the fortification would stand until 1820—even as Mobile passed between the French, the British, the Spanish, and finally the Americans. Fort Charlotte (so-named under British rule) was finally demolished soon after the United States took possession of Mobile, a casualty of progress as the city's new owners expanded the street grid. The version of Fort Charlotte that stands downtown today is a ⅘ scale reproduction built in conjunction with the U.S. Bicentennial in 1976—a way for the city to celebrate an anniversary to which it had little direct connection.

Mobile itself would grow slowly during these early centuries, inhibited by its relative isolation, by the compromised potential of its distant and vulnerable port, and by the explosive growth of nearby New Orleans, which sits at a much more providential location on the off-ramp of North America's original interstate highway, the Mississippi-Ohio-Missouri River system.

The United States seized Mobile from Spain at the outbreak of the War of 1812. During the first half of 1813, the U.S. built its first coastal fortress at Mobile Point. Guarding the narrow pass into Mobile Bay, Fort Bowyer was largely improvised from local materials—sand, stone, and timber. It was fan-shaped and armed with no more than fourteen guns.

Mottled sunlight streams through the vegetation now thoroughly in command of Fort Morgan's parapet.

There's a reason, aside from its somewhat esoteric origins, that the War of 1812 is little remembered in the United States. Broadly speaking, it was not the nation's finest military moment.

During the course of the war, U.S. forces were met with one clumsy defeat after another. In mid-September of 1814, the British sought to capture Mobile—not for the city's own modest strategic value, but as a jumping-off point for an overland campaign that would cut American access to New Orleans.

A mixed force of about 120 Royal Marines and Native American allies landed nine miles east of Mobile Point with the aim of carrying out a diversionary assault on Fort Bowyer. These were handily repulsed by Fort Bowyer's 160 defenders.

The primary attack followed the next day, at a moment when the wind and tide were favorable to ships heading into the bay. Four British ships, each with arms greater than the total number fielded by the American defenders, opened fire on Fort Bowyer. In the turmoil of the assault, the HMS *Hermes* ran aground in the shallow waters off Mobile Point, directly under the guns of Fort Bowyer. To prevent any American salvage operations of her wreck, *Hermes* was scuttled—set alight and blown to splinters when the blaze reached the ship's magazine.

The British withdrew in defeat. The First Battle of Fort Bowyer proved that U.S. victories during the War of 1812 could be just as clumsy as their defeats.

Like night and day—seen through the open end of a cave-like passageway within the fort's walls, the brilliance of the sunlit parade is utterly dazzling. Historically, of course, most all light at Fort Gaines would have been natural, supplemented with oil lamps or candlelight.

The view of the oft-contested strait between Mobile Point and Dauphin Island as seen from Fort Gaines, a fort that wouldn't exist until some forty years after the War of 1812.

Having grown up in a country quite enamored of its own military might, in a family with a long tradition of military service dating back to the settling of Puritan Massachusetts, I am constantly in awe of the number of battles in which the outcome is decided not by superior arms or strategy, but by sheer happenstance—by some accidental brush with a natural feature, by some variable for which there was no real way to account. Quite apart from glory, valor, or cunning—how often are the winners chosen by something so banal as an inconvenient sandbar? The British withdrew.

And so, the First Battle of Fort Bowyer proved that U.S. victories during the War of 1812 could be just as clumsy as the nation's defeats. Such is war.

The primary lesson learned from this fleeting engagement was that fortifying the point had worked. Even if the *coup de gras* halting the British advance had been a shallow, silted channel—what had nudged the *Hermes* onto that shoal in the first place, hm? The feeble guns of Fort Bowyer, that's what!

General Andrew Jackson, charged with the defense of New Orleans, saw clearly what the British had intended to do at Mobile and ordered Fort Bowyer reinforced with several hundred additional men. Satisfied, though not personally present in Alabama to surveil it himself, Jackson predicted, "10,000 men cannot take it."

Had history proven him right, the Second Battle of Fort Bowyer might be cited alongside other examples of Andrew Jackson's bold derring-do. As it happened, Jackson's confidence turned out to be misplaced. His prophecy, in this case, looks rather more like bluster.

The exact site of Fort Bowyer—an earthen and timber structure on Mobile Point, occupied for only a short period during the War of 1812—is unknown, its ruins likely churned and displaced by later construction projects.

In early February 1815, the British returned in still greater force, landing more than 1,000 men who, sustaining only modest losses, constructed formidable siege works on the fort's eastern end in the space of several days. The Royal Navy blockaded the pass to the west, and Fort Bowyer was promptly beset under a blistering barrage from both sides.

The British commander called upon the defenders of the fort to surrender in the face of overwhelming firepower—to avoid the needless loss of human life. His American counterpart readily agreed, stipulating one condition: that the formal transfer occur the following morning "as so many of his men had got drunk" while staring down the barrel of their own seemingly imminent doom.

The victorious British were making preparations to move on the city of Mobile, when word arrived from afar that a treaty had been signed. The war between Britain and the United States was over and had been for a month even before the second assault on Fort Bowyer had even commenced. The whole drama had all been for naught—the siege, the bombardment, the loss of life, the hangovers—all of it!

The Second Battle of Fort Bowyer proved to be the final engagement of the War of 1812.

The Treaty of Ghent affirmed the U.S. annexation of Mobile from the Spanish. The interior of Alabama, previously landlocked in a protracted game of geopolitical chess, suddenly had a direct maritime link to the markets of the industrializing Northeast and Europe.

This vast swath of real estate, prime for the cultivation and export of cotton and other cash crops, stood as a unified territory for the first time—that is, save for the substantial population of Native Americans who had the misfortune of claiming this appealing countryside as their ancestral homeland. Over the next generation, the state of Alabama would be wrested from the hands of the Choctaw and the Chickasaw, the Creek and the Cherokee by Anglo settlers and squatters, backed by the full military, economic, and legal force of the United States government.

Slavery grew as the fortunes of Native Americans waned. The first 120 enslaved Africans had arrived in Mobile aboard a French warship in 1721, just two decades after the city's founding. Under the aegis of the United States, Mobile was home to the state's largest slave auction house, facilitating the domestic market in human stock even after the international slave trade was banned by federal law in 1807.

When Alabama was admitted into the Union in 1819, more than thirty percent of the new state's population was enslaved, accounting for approximately 120,000 involuntary residents. When Alabama seceded in 1861, this percentage had risen to forty-five percent, or roughly 435,080 slaves—many of whom had entered the state through the port of Mobile, arriving from Africa, the Caribbean, or the East Coast.

From March to July 1837, Fort Morgan served as an internment camp for 3,000 Creek civilians. While the men of the tribe were away, serving in the U.S. Army during the Second Seminole War, their families were removed from their homes and imprisoned here to await deportation westward. Without adequate water or sanitation, 117 Creek died at Fort Morgan.

In 1824, the new Alabama state legislature established a commission to improve Mobile Bay for shipping. Over the coming years, largely at federal expense, Mobile Bay's shipping channel was dredged, linking the state directly to oceangoing ship traffic for the first time. This only served to increase the economic and strategic value of the city. By 1860, Mobile was the second largest port on the Gulf Coast, moving more cotton than any other port in the world except New Orleans.

It was during this period that a federal commission, as part of an ambitious plan for nationwide coastal defense known as the Third System, identified Mobile Bay as one of the top five most vulnerable ports in the country. Despite its ordinal name, the Third System was essentially the first truly coordinated national defense plan in the history of the United States—its first hesitant step on the not-at-all-preordained path toward its twentieth century status as a world-class military power.

The military lesson learned and applied after the Second Battle of Fort Bowyer was that an *ad hoc* fortification of sand and timber was unequal to the task of defending a port as valuable as Mobile Bay. Something more deliberate was in order—the Third System offered a carefully considered rejoinder, incorporating the best military technology of the day.

Such was the origin of Forts Morgan and Gaines.

The First System of coastal defense was comprised mostly of low fortifications built of earth and wood, hastily executed during the Revolutionary War. The Second System, a hodgepodge of casemated brick forts, was developed without any great urgency between 1789 and 1812 and proved woefully inadequate during the conflict that erupted in that year. The Third System, built between 1816 and 1867, consisted of 42 masonry forts incorporating the latest military concepts of the day.

Built between 1819 and 1834, Fort Morgan cost $1,026,777.41. This included U.S. government leases of the region's enslaved persons—the men, women, and children who would ultimately fire and lay a substantial portion of the 30,000,000 bricks composing the fort's main structure.

3

SIEGE-WEARY FORT MORGAN

Fort Morgan is hidden from view by a gently sloping man-made ridge known as a glacis. Any attacking enemy would have to cross this broad space without cover, under fire from the guns of the fort. This earthen embankment also absorbed the enemy's artillery fire, sparing the fort's curtain walls from direct bombardment.

A visitor to Mobile Point can't really see Fort Morgan. Not all at once, or in one sweeping vista, no matter where they stand. From a distance, it's almost completely invisible. And of course, like almost everything else about the fort, this invisibility is by design.

Fort Morgan sits behind a broad glacis—an earthen slope cleared of all obstructions, gently rising until level with the fort's curtain walls, from which it is separated by a wide ditch. The glacis is a custom-made no man's land compelling any attacking force into the open and uphill, exposed under full view of the fort's guns. This slope also shielded Fort Morgan from any direct artillery fire originating from an enemy's land-based guns. Instead of shattering the fort's brick walls, the ballistic force of these shells would, in theory, be absorbed harmlessly into the earthen hillside.

Same general effect, incidentally, for any camera attempting to shoot the fort in the twenty-first century. I tried, but short of a drone, the best perspective on Fort Morgan's size is just how hard it is to photograph.

Built between 1819 and 1834, Fort Morgan reduced two separate federal contractors to financial ruin. These were men who thought, in their hubris, that they could bring a construction project as grand as Fort Morgan to completion under budget and on time. They were both from up north, more familiar with urban areas like Boston and New York, cities which in this period hummed with commerce and industry. Each failed to understand, until it was too late and the ink had dried on their contracts, just how preindustrial the antebellum South was.

Then these ill-fated contractors arrived at Mobile Point—a frontier in every sense of the word—and realized just how difficult it would be to source the bricks and other materials needed to construct a massive, two-tiered fort, complete with outworks and a three-tiered citadel at its heart.

By 1821, these successive contractors were dead—both from diseases contracted or exacerbated by the balmy conditions on Alabama's Gulf Coast. Private enterprise had failed, and the U.S. Army Corps of Engineers assumed full responsibility for the completion of Fort Morgan. The more formidable of the two forts conceived for Mobile Bay, Fort Morgan sat directly adjacent the deepest section of the shipping channel, to which all contemporary warships of any significant draught or menace to Mobile would be compelled to hew.

The fort was finally completed in 1834, the date inscribed above its lustrous granite sally port. If no expense was spared on its construction, then many expenses were spared in its cantonment. The threat of war with some European power, seemingly inevitable during the Napoleonic era in which the Third System was conceived, felt far more remote by the 1830s. The general plan was to station within this massive fort only a token caretaker force which could then be reinforced in times of trouble.

In 1842, less than a decade after its dedication, a young William Tecumseh Sherman was stationed at Fort Morgan. In his memoirs, he described a fort already neglected and seemingly on its way to seed:

> This fort had not been occupied by troops for many years, was very dirty, and we found little or no stores there. Taking advantage of one of the engineer schooners engaged in bringing materials for the fort, I went up to Mobile city, procured all essentials for the troops, and returned to the post. We proceeded to put the post in as good order as possible; had regular guard-mounting and parades, but little drill. We found

This Parrott rifle was one of the most advanced artillery pieces available during the Civil War. Invented in 1860 by U.S. Army Captain Robert Parker Parrott, it could hurl a 100-pound projectile up to 6,900 yards with a degree of power and accuracy largely unattainable by the Confederates. Though the Rebels developed a few fine rifles of their own, they struggled to produce them at scale, even as the Union blockade made it difficult to obtain comparable British-made artillery.

Following the shambolic War of 1812, Congress ordered a comprehensive national plan for seacoast defense. The initial round of forts in this so-called Third System, which included Fort Morgan, were designed by Simon Bernard, a skilled military engineer banished from post-Napoleonic France. His French nomenclature continues to grace U.S. fortifications —this is the postern tunnel, the only way past the glacis without facing a hail of defensive fire over the top.

Left: Fort Morgan's postern tunnel was originally capped on either end by heavy iron-reinforced doors hung from these massive hinges.

Below: The sand floor of Fort Morgan's postern tunnel was replaced by a paved surface embedded with rails (since removed, but still visible under the sally port) sometime around the turn of the twentieth century, the better to supply a new generation of gun batteries constructed within.

magnificent fishing with the seine on the outer beach, and sometimes in a single haul we would take ten or fifteen barrels of the best kind of fish, embracing pompinos, red-fish, snappers, etc.

At least the fishing was good. Probably even better than it is today.

But in the tumultuous middle decades of the nineteenth century, this idyll could not persist, even at remote Fort Morgan.

Early in the morning on January 4, 1861, the Alabama State Militia relieved the modest Federal garrison stationed here. At sunrise, 159 years almost to the minute before this photo was taken, the Alabama state flag replaced the Stars and Stripes

Upon exiting the postern tunnel, a visitor comes face-to-face with an unusually splendid sally port, displaying the fort's name and its dedication date in finely hewn granite.

Fort Morgan is a pentagonal fort with two primary seacoast walls bearing on the channel, two secondary seacoast walls facing the Gulf and Bay, and a fifth wall defending the landward approach. It is protected by five bastions and a dry moat, making a direct assault on Fort Morgan, at best, a pyrrhic victory for any enemy—the only practical way to take the fort was by siege.

above Fort Morgan. One Alabama militiaman wrote, with a bravado typical of those early, heady days, " ... we are ready to receive any distinguished strangers the Government may see fit to send on a visit to us."

Across the channel, Fort Gaines was seized under similar circumstances, with nary a shot fired. It's almost like the fishing, sunning, napping federal garrisons of these forts couldn't feel the national tide shifting so furiously around them. Alabama formally seceded from the Union a week later, and the Confederacy was proclaimed a month after that.

It was to be a new era in which Alabama would seek its own fortune, free of any Federal encumbrance—and the heart of any future prosperity certainly beat in Mobile Bay, the state's commercial center. Mobile had to be defended at all costs.

The Rebels promptly set about buttressing the defenses of Mobile Bay. Confederate forces completed construction on the long-delayed, still languishing Fort Gaines. They also improved the eastern, landward defenses of Fort Morgan, building additional earthen redoubts and entrenchments to slow any prospective Union attempts at retaking the fort.

This view from the parapet shows the glacis, behind which is the covert way, a first line of defense outside of the fort's dry moat. Should this position become untenable, Fort Morgan's defenders could retreat into the fort proper, sealing the sally port behind them. From this high position, sharpshooters and artillery crews would still command a clear range of fire around the fort.

The counterscarp is the wall of the moat opposite the fort's outer wall, itself sometimes called a scarp or curtain wall. Shots fired from loopholes and embrasures in the scarp would ricochet off the brick counterscarp, increasing the hazard for any enemy soldiers who infiltrated the dry moat.

The cunette is a narrow ditch surrounding the fort providing drainage for the dry moat.

Through embrasures in the fort's bastions, defenders could use specialized cannons called flank howitzers to fire canisters of shot parallel the fort's walls. Canister burst when fired, creating a deadly hail of grape-sized pellets capable of shredding the flesh of any man in their path. This moat would serve as an awful place to die for any invader unlucky enough to find his way over the glacis.

The fort's northeast bastion appears in much the same state as it might have during the siege of Fort Morgan in August 1864. The gun seen here is a flank howitzer, one of the most ferocious weapons the fort's defenders might wield against a *coup de main*.

Like most forts in the Third System, Fort Morgan is named for a Revolutionary War hero. In this case, the namesake is Brigadier General Daniel Morgan, a gifted tactician known for his clever battlefield tactics, especially at the Battle of Cowpens (1781). The sally port was originally sealed with heavy doors entering into a chamber lined with loopholes, one of the fort's final lines of defense.

Fort Morgan's parade was once home to a three-story, ten-sided citadel, which housed the fortification's garrison. This building was embellished with fine architectural details in the vein of fort's surviving granite sally port. The citadel was irreparably damaged during an artillery barrage that culminated in the fort's ultimate surrender to Union forces on August 23, 1864.

Upon entering the parade, one begins to fully appreciate the scale of Fort Morgan. Each of its five sides has seven bomb-resistant casemates—vaulted brick arches supporting the tremendous weight of the barbette tier above, from which crews fired heavy seacoast artillery.

The steep stairwells flanking either end of the casemates are peculiar to Fort Morgan. More often, Third System forts featured at least one ramp, a shallower stairwell, or a secondary magazine on a higher level. With great effort, men moved incredibly heavy cannonballs and powder by hand up these punishing steps to supply the gun crews above.

The forts were also supplemented by a cross channel minefield which allowed only a narrow passage directly under the heaviest guns of Fort Morgan. Finally, a brand new steam-powered ironclad, the CSS *Tennessee*, competitive with any vessel fielded by the Union, was stationed in Mobile Bay, ready to harass any warship brazen enough to challenge the formidable combined might of Forts Morgan and Gaines.

The guns of Forts Morgan and Gaines also provided cover for ships running the Union blockade of Mobile, which lasted from the early days of the war all the way until 1865. This was part of the larger—and largely successful—Federal Anaconda Plan, which aimed to constrict and constrain the foreign trade upon which the mostly preindustrial Confederate States of America so desperately relied.

In this secondary mission, the forts at Mobile Bay enjoyed a very high rate of success—nineteen of twenty-one inbound vessels successfully defied Union vessels wary of coming under fire from these forts at too close a range. All seventeen outbound attempts were successful.

The Civil War had been a game of endurance from the outset—an open question of whether an outgunned and increasingly impoverished Confederacy could muster enough determination to outlast the expansive resources of an industrialized Union.

A 7-inch Brooke rifle on display at Fort Morgan, similar to ones deployed at the fort during its Civil War heyday. Such rifles were the Confederacy's answer to the Union's far more numerous Parrott rifle. Both guns could fire a projectile with greater force and accuracy than traditional smoothbore cannon—a development which, coupled with imminent advances in metallurgy, would soon bring into question the efficacy of masonry forts like Morgan and Gaines.

The pintle, a durable iron pivot, was the axis around which a several-ton piece of artillery rotated.

Typically, the rear end of the barbette carriage stood on castors which rode on a curved iron track, embedded in the rounded white stones seen here. This allowed for relative ease of movement as crews of eight loaded, positioned, and fired each gun. Farragut's fleet wielded 199 shipborne guns, compared to twenty-six at Fort Gaines and forty-six at Fort Morgan.

Each bastion of Fort Morgan provided firing positions for up to five artillery pieces. Note the contoured brick surfaces of the fort's terreplein—designed to divert rainwater away from the guns and into cisterns buried beneath the parade where it was stored for daily use.

The North's population—and by extension, its productive workforce and military reserves—continued to grow apace, fueled by immigration even during the darkest days of the war.

By summer of 1864, the contest's ultimate outcome was becoming increasingly clear to any sober-eyed observer. Even Britain, the South's erstwhile partner-in-crime in defiance of the Union blockade, had turned bearish on the Confederacy's long-term prospects. The Union Navy now commanded the Mississippi River, closing the South's largest port at New Orleans, cleaving the eastern portion of the Confederacy from its western frontier. The Union Army of the Tennessee under Fort Morgan-alum General William T. Sherman commenced a siege of Atlanta, and the Army of the Potomac under Ulysses S. Grant set its sights on the Rebel capital at Richmond.

The tide of the war had shifted irrevocably, and Union Rear Admiral David Farragut—a giant fit to stand shoulder-to-shoulder with Grant and Sherman in the annals of Civil War lore—was set to ride that tide into Mobile Bay, one of the last major ports remaining in Confederate hands.

Consulting nautical charts, Farragut planned his assault for dawn on a morning when the flood tide would carry his ships swiftly through the gantlet of Confederate defenses. The 180 mines in the channel—known in the parlance of the day as torpedoes, before the self-propelled device we think of today had been invented—forced his fourteen ships to make this passage in narrow formation and at point-blank range under the guns of Fort Morgan.

Even during Fort Morgan's prime, weeding the gaps in the masonry fort was a perpetual chore – the terreplein, the banquette (a raised firing position, partially visible here), the parapet (a masonry wall shielding all action on the second level from enemy fire), even the casemates themselves, required regular attention, lest some irksome root system pry the structure apart before an enemy's artillery fire ever found their range.

Drainage issues have plagued the fort's upper level since the 1830s, impacting the integrity of the casemates below. Various remedies have been employed beneath the brick terreplein—layers of compacted stone, sand fill, lead sheets—as the fort's caretakers have worked to plug leaks and channel rainwater toward drains like this one.

These drainage problems have also destabilized the parapet, an issue to be addressed in the course of ongoing conservation efforts. The seepage is worst on the fort's east side, which also took the brunt of the Union's bombardment during the siege of August 1864.

Farragut's attempt to run the defenses of Mobile Bay would be led by four ironclads—the *Tecumseh*, followed by the *Manhattan*, *Winnebago*, and the *Chickasaw*. Protected by their heavy armor, these state-of-the-art ships were far more resistant to artillery fire than were the more numerous wooden ships comprising the balance of the Union armada. Accordingly, they were to cover the fleet's right flank, closest to the guns of Fort Morgan.

Once clear of the narrow passage between Fort Morgan on the right and the submerged torpedoes on the left, these ironclads would engage the four Confederate warships stationed inside Mobile Bay. They were to concentrate on the most formidable of these Rebel ships—the Confederate ironclad ram *Tennessee*.

As a further precaution against calamity, Farragut ordered that the fourteen wooden ships under his command be lashed together in pairs so that if the steam engine of one were damaged in the inevitable hail of enemy fire, it could still be towed from harm's way by its partner.

In an era before aerial reconnaissance, the only vantage point from which to command such an elaborate maneuver was from the rigging of his flagship, the

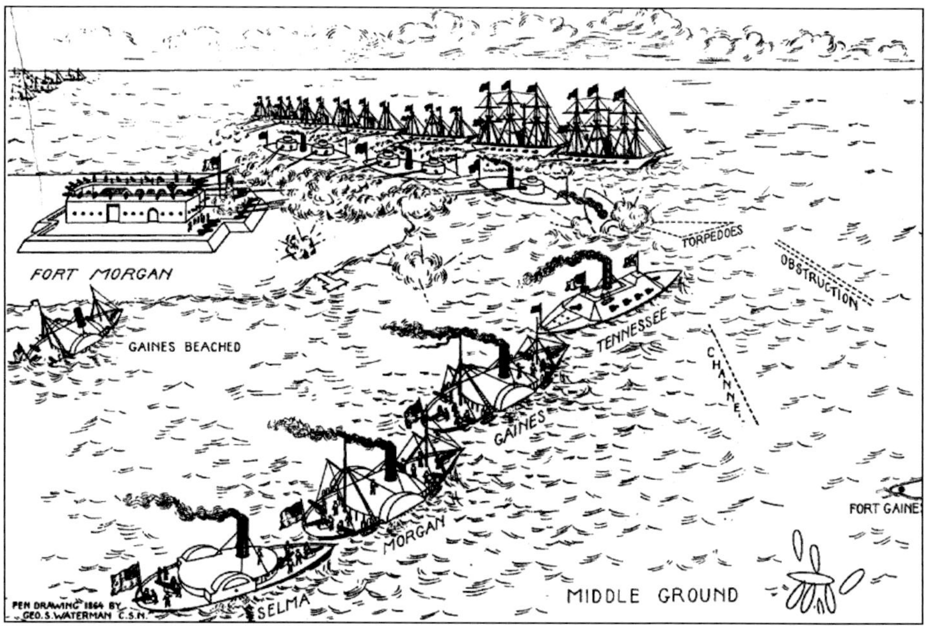

This pen drawing completed by George Waterman, a Confederate sailor present during the Battle of Mobile Bay, depicts the foundering USS *Tecumseh*. The wooden vessels of the Union fleet, lashed in pairs, proceed into the minefield, while the surviving Union ironclads return fire against Fort Morgan. The diagram in the lower right corner indicates how the Union fleet eventually ganged up to disable the CSS *Tennessee*. [*National Park Service*]

USS *Hartford*. Farragut was strapped in, lest the sudden concussion of enemy bombardment cause him to plummet to his death on the unforgiving deck below.

Despite the drama inherent in this scene, Farragut was no swashbuckling young man. At the age of sixty-three, nearing the end of a distinguished naval career, he was quite somber about the long odds aligned against his success in the face of such fierce Confederate defenses. The night before, he had written to his wife:

> Off Mobile, August 4, 1864.
>
> My dearest Wife: I write and leave this letter for you. I am going into Mobile in the morning, if God is my leader, as I hope he is, and in him I place my trust. If he thinks it is the proper place for me to die, I am ready to submit to his will in that as in all other things. My great mortification is that my vessels, the ironclads, were not ready to have gone in yesterday. The army landed last night, and are in full view of us this morning, and the Tecumseh has not yet arrived from Pensacola.
>
> God bless and preserve you, my darling, and my dear boy, if anything should happen to me...
>
> Your devoted and affectionate husband, who never for one moment forgot his love, duty, or fidelity to you, his devoted and best of wives,
>
> D. G. Farragut.

And so it was, on the morning of August 5, with the unyielding forces of nature—the wind and the current—at their backs, Farragut's armada entered the channel.

As the Admiral expected, the Confederate gun crews stationed behind Fort Morgan's parapet greeted them with a series of devastating volleys. One Rebel recalled of the subsequent fusillade, "The roar of cannon was like one continuous peal of thunder, deafening to the extreme."

Another witness painted a withering picture of pure mayhem on the deck below Farragut's high perch: "Shot after shot crushed into the *Hartford*, mowing down men, deluging the decks with blood and scattering mangled fragments of humanity so thickly that it was difficult to stand on the deck."

Yikes.

And then things went to hell.

The ironclad *Tecumseh*, which had arrived in the nick of time to lead the Union procession, suddenly broke formation, moving westward in the channel in what was likely a premature attempt to engage the CSS *Tennessee*. Crossing the path of the wooden vessels she was meant to shield, bound for glory in a bedlam of her own making, the *Tecumseh* instead struck a torpedo. Only twenty-one of her 114-man crew would escape with their lives, but Farragut had bigger problems.

Dead in the water, listing at a sickening angle, her screw turning menacingly in the air, and sinking rapidly under the burden of her heavy armor—the disabled *Tecumseh* now blocked safe passage for the entire Union armada which was fast coming up behind her in the narrow channel.

With his vulnerable wooden ships stalled directly under the guns of Fort Morgan, the entire assault threatened to devolve into a deadly fiasco. Farragut had to act quickly.

Over the din of the raging battle, he barked an order to the captain of the *Hartford*—with the *Metacomet* lashed clumsily to her side, they were to proceed westward, directly into the minefield. The ten wooden ships behind them were to follow. Boldly, perhaps recklessly, they would take their chances against the same undetectable explosives which had just sunk the mighty *Tecumseh*.

But what was the alternative? Was it better to face certain doom—as Confederate gunners positioned safely behind Fort Morgan's parapet picked them off one by one?

"Damn the torpedoes, full speed ahead!" Farragut is supposed to have shouted in reply to his officers' protestations—a veritable Hollywood action hero one-liner, a cool and pithy retort in the face of danger. It's probably a muddle of what he actually said, but why spoil a good story trying to reconstruct words lost in the rumble of the cannons?

An anchor from Farragut's flagship, the USS *Hartford*, is displayed at Fort Gaines. The *Hartford* survived the Battle of Mobile Bay and remained in service until 1926. Franklin Roosevelt wanted the decommissioned ship for a proposed naval museum in Washington, DC, but these plans died with the late president. Instead, neglected, she sank in her berth in 1954. Various *Hartford* relics are on display around the nation.

A relic of the era of wooden ships, this hot shot furnace serviced a specialized battery outside the southwest bastion of Fort Morgan. It was used to heat cannonballs to a glowing orange temperature, the better to ignite their targets upon impact. These were promptly fired at ships both during the Battle of Mobile Bay and as cover for smugglers during the blockade preceding it.

Fortunately for Farragut and his men, no other mines detonated that day. It was later estimated that only about eighteen in the field of 180 were even functional. Seawater had swamped the remainder, a clear demonstration of just how new and imperfect a technology submersible mines were in 1864.

In any event, the battered Union armada entered the bay and made quick work of the small Confederate fleet stationed there. The Rebel ships were neutralized within three hours of Farragut's initial approach, but victory came at a heavy price. Confederate casualties during the naval engagement totaled only thirty-two, while the Union force racked up slightly more than ten times that many losses—mostly during the initial run through the channel.

And still, their mission was incomplete. While the forts remained safely in Confederate hands, the Union fleet could not make any credible claim to control of Mobile Bay.

Accordingly, Farragut's attention now turned to Fort Powell, a modest earthen redoubt built by the Confederates to guard a shallow "back door" to Mobile Bay through Pass au Heron. Hopelessly outmatched, its defenders abandoned their posts promptly, spiking their guns and wading ashore in retreat toward Mobile.

In the modern day, any trace of Fort Powell is long gone. Given how quickly the position was yielded, it's fair enough to question the extent to which it was ever there.

The tower and the museum in the foreground are new, but David Farragut would probably still recognize the scene of his triumph: the view from Mobile Bay just north of Fort Morgan. Confederate guns fired 491 rounds during his daring run through the channel but failed to sink a single Union ship. The USS *Tecumseh* sank after it struck a submerged mine at the very right edge of this photo.

The Confederate ironclad *Tennessee*—designed to ram wooden ships, gouging their hulls below the waterline—surrendered just north of Fort Gaines, not far from this modern natural gas rig. After action reports reveal a great deal of interest in the captured vessel from Union naval commanders who hoped to glean insights from the Confederate approach to the still emerging technology of armored warships.

Next page: With a force that ultimately numbered 5,500, the Union Army tightened their siege lines around Fort Morgan until they were firing from within 200 yards of the glacis. From this range, field artillery like this 30-pounder Parrott rifle could strike the ramparts of the fort, dismounting Confederate guns and casting shattered bricks high into the air. "When a shell strikes, they shower in every direction," remembered a Confederate defender.

The commander of Fort Gaines capitulated several days later, offering similarly limited resistance. This surrender was greeted with great acclaim from Union officers who praised his rational assessment of the situation.

It was met with commensurately great scorn from General Richard L. Page, in charge of the Confederate garrison inside Fort Morgan. Under his defiant leadership, the 600 men there settled in for a siege against the full brunt of the Union forces amassed in Mobile Bay.

On August 9, with Fort Gaines secure, 400 Union soldiers came ashore some miles east of Mobile Point, manhandling their heavy cannon and mortars over sandy dunes. After establishing siege lines to the east of Fort Morgan, they heaped a blistering salvo on the fort and its outworks. Simultaneously, Farragut's ships battered Fort Morgan from their position in the bay.

By August 16, the Confederate defenders had abandoned the outer defenses, retreating behind the curtain walls of Fort Morgan. The U.S. Army moved its mortars to within 500 yards of the fort and rained down an even more concentrated hell from above.

Whether or not General Page wished to admit it, the end was near.

A Union artillery officer described the devastating final bombardment Fort Morgan, a collaboration between the Union Navy and Army which commenced on August 22, "The gunners seemed to perform their duty with wild enthusiasm, stripping themselves of all superfluous clothing, and blackened, begrimed with the smoke, and dirt, and sweat of battle, their eyes sparkling through the hazy air ... they might well have been taken for so many Vulcans forging thunderbolts for the gods."

Mortars similar to this modern reproduction were used by the Union Army to lob 8-inch, 44-pound explosive shells in a high arc over the walls of Fort Morgan. At a range of 800 yards, about half of the shells fired from such a weapon would fall within a 50-yard radius of the target, making nearly every shot a direct hit on something within the fort.

Walking the terreplein of Fort Morgan today, it's easy enough to falsely attribute all the ravages of time to the Union bombardment. In fact, within hours of the Confederate surrender, the Union Army had catalogued all damage sustained by their guns – the opening stage of an extensive program of repairs that saw the fort thoroughly restored and battle-ready within months.

Recalling the sorry condition of siege-weary Fort Morgan on the evening of August 22, General Page reported:

> At daylight the fleet was reported moving up to encircle us, and shortly its batteries (in conjunction with those on land, which numbered thirty-six (36) guns and mortars) opened a furious fire, which came from almost every point of the compass, and continued unabated throughout the day, culminating in increased force at sundown; after which the heavy calibres and mortars kept it up during the night.
>
> This fire disabled all the heavy guns, save two, which did not bear on the land approach, partially breached the walls in several places, and cut up the fort to such extent as to make the whole work a mere mass of debris. Their mortar practice was accurate.
>
> Early in the night the woodwork of the citadel was fired by the mortar shells and burned furiously for some hours, the enemy during the conflagration pouring in his missiles with increased vigor. With great efforts the fire was arrested and prevented extending around near the magazines, which would have been in imminent danger of explosion.

Should Fort Morgan's magazines (containing enough powder to resist months of siege) ignite, the entire fort would likely have been leveled, killing most every man inside. In desperation, Page ordered around 60,000 pounds of powder doused.

Robert B. Tarpley, 1st Tennessee Heavy Artillery, recalled, "This was a terrible job. The powder was in kegs. These we had to roll under the flames of the citadel and knock the heads in, then pour the contents in the cisterns. All this time the enemy kept up a continual fire from land and sea. The shells were bursting all around

Casemates on the fort's first level supported the terrific weight of the heavy artillery above. The space inside was typically utilized in the day-to-day operations of a working fort, with different compartments running the gamut from kitchen to blacksmith's workshop.

This doorway, at the base of the eastern bastion, leads into one of the powder magazines. Each bastion was filled with a tremendous volume of earth, creating a shielded position for the magazine, which had to be protected from enemy fire at all costs. In the end, this was not nearly shelter enough. Some thirty tons of powder had to be doused to avert catastrophe during the siege.

us. By one o'clock we had all the powder under water. There was not enough dry powder to shoot a musket."

Page was a true believer in the righteousness of the Confederate cause, which certainly compounded the difficulty of his next decision:

> At daylight on the 23d (all my powder had then been destroyed) the citadel was again set on fire in several places by shells, and had burned until it was consumed.
>
> The report made to me now was that the casemates, which had been rendered as safe as possible for the men, some had been breached, ... another shot on them would bring down the walls of their company quarters... so that a resumption or the severe fire from the enemy would in all likelihood inflict great loss of life, there being no bombproof in the fort. The enemy's approach was very near the glacis, my guns and powder had all been destroyed, my means of defense gone, the citadel, nearly the entire quartermaster stores, and a portion of the commissariat burned by the enemy's shells. It was evident the fort could hold out but a few hours longer under a renewed bombardment. The only question was: Hold it for this time, gain the éclat, and sustain the loss of life from the falling of the walls, or save life and capitulate?

Winter sun streams through the remains of an enclosed casemate, throwing its intricate archways into elegant relief.

On August 23, 1864, after a siege of two weeks, Fort Morgan surrendered. The United States was the effective master of Mobile Bay once more, and one of the last Confederate lifelines to the outside world had fallen. Farragut's official dispatches to Washington paint the scathing portrait of a Rebel commander surrendering not only his post, but his dignity and honor along with it:

> I regret to state that after the assembling of the rebel officers at the appointed hour, 2 p.m., for the surrender outside the fort, it was discovered on an examination of the interior that most of the guns were spiked, many of the gun carriages wantonly injured, and arms, ammunition, and provisions, etc., destroyed, and that there was every reason to believe that this had been done after the white flag had been raised.
>
> It was also discovered that General Page and several of his officers had no swords to deliver up, and, further, that some of those which were surrendered had been broken.
>
> The whole conduct of the officers of Fort Gaines and Fort Morgan presents such a striking contrast in moral principle that I cannot fail to remark upon it. Colonel Anderson, who commanded the former, finding himself in a position perfectly untenable, and encumbered with a superfluous number of conscripts, many of whom were mere boys, determined to surrender a fort which he could not defend, and in this determination was supported by all his officers save one, but from the moment he hoisted the white flag he scrupulously kept everything intact, and in that condition delivered it over, whilst General Page and his officers, with a childish spitefulness, destroyed the guns which they had said they would defend to the last, but which they never defended at all, and threw away or broke those weapons which they had not the manliness to use against their enemies, for Fort Morgan never fired a gun after the commencement of the bombardment, and the advanced pickets of our army were actually on its glacis.

This tranquil vista must have been something else entirely at sunrise on the morning of August 23, 1864—smoldering, cratered, with siege-rattled rebels dashing to-and-fro to spike the fort's remaining guns, as the white flag of surrender fluttered over the parapet.

Of course, not even Simon Bernard, Fort Morgan's original architect, thought that it—or any fort—could withstand bombardment indefinitely. His best estimate was that Fort Morgan would be able to repel a siege of approximately three weeks before a friendly force might arrive to relieve the pressure. As it happened, Fort Morgan fell to Union forces a few days short of that three-week mark.

The fact of the matter was that in August 1864, there was simply no friendly force available to reinforce the fort's defenders. The defensive walls around the broader Confederacy were caving in as surely and completely as those of Fort Morgan.

Despite this, Fort Morgan had proven almost completely ineffectual in carrying out its original mission—the defense of Mobile Bay.

Fort Morgan's guns had failed to seriously damage any one of the Union ships that crossed its line of fire at point blank range. These were moving under steam power, with the tide and the wind at their back, and some were clad in iron. A stationary fort, even one equipped with dozens of guns along its primary seacoast walls, could little hope to stop such swift-moving, well-armored craft.

But most ominously—the Union Army and Navy at Mobile Point were equipped with rifled artillery, capable of firing shells more accurately and with greater force than the conventional smoothbore weapons in use when Fort Morgan was conceived. Given a clear line of fire and a stable enough platform, these new weapons could rattle the brittle masonry walls of any Third System fort, just as Page had described in justifying his surrender. All the while, the guns of Fort Morgan had been unable to deliver more than a glancing blow to the Union's ironclads. Even though the bugs were still being worked out, the new-fangled minefield had proven much more effective on this front.

In the end, Fort Morgan didn't so much fall; it revealed itself as the museum piece it was well on its way to becoming.

Elsewhere, the Union Army was engaged in extensive efforts to take Atlanta and Richmond. Without significant reinforcements of their own, the Union contingent newly in possession of Forts Morgan and Gaines dared not make an attempt on the city of Mobile. But that didn't matter much.

The Union's most important objective in Mobile Bay had been achieved—blockade runners could no longer operate from Alabama. For all intents and purposes, the city of Mobile had been neutralized as a Confederate asset.

This gun emplacement at Fort Morgan is rusted along its metal seams, but otherwise retains most of its original luster. Even after nearly two centuries of battle and exposure, it ranks as an impressive piece of stonework.

4

FORT GAINES: A FATE WRITTEN IN SHATTERED BRICK

Fort Gaines was originally planned as an exact twin of Fort Morgan. Construction began in 1821, but concerns about the quality of work done by contracted labor led to its abandonment. In the 1850s, building commenced on a new version of the fort based on a design by General Joseph Totten, Chief Engineer of the United States Army.

Fort Gaines lies on the eastern end of Dauphin Island, just a short cruise away from Fort Morgan at Mobile Point. In the modern day, an efficient, regular ferry service operates from piers mere feet from the entrances of the respective forts. The journey parallels the historic Confederate minefield, not far from where the wreck of the USS *Tecumseh* still rests at the bottom of the channel. From the ferry's open-air observation deck, with the chill wind in your face, you can roleplay your own "Damn the torpedoes!" moment with all the gusto of Tom Petty.

Both forts are well-maintained, but the compact Fort Gaines is the neater, better preserved of the two, which makes sense. As alluded to in the last chapter, Fort Gaines slipped into Union hands with almost no resistance and nary a shot fired.

On August 3, 1864, two days before the Battle of Mobile Bay, Union forces under Major General Gordon Granger landed near the western end of Dauphin Island, about seven miles march from Fort Gaines. Over the next 24 hours, his 1,500 men advanced steadily, encountering Confederate resistance that could be characterized as either quixotic or desperate, depending on your perspective. Union Colonel John M. Wilson recalled:

> In moving up, our forces captured a battalion of boys, varying from 12 to 16 years old, the sons of the leading citizens of Mobile. ... the [boys] seemed to know nothing of the art of skirmishing, and, instead of seeking cover where it could be found, invariably stood bravely to receive and deliver the fire. Several were wounded before it was found that they were boys, and, soon after, the whole battalion was captured ... wisely paroled ... and sent ... to their anxious mothers in Mobile.

After dispensing in short order with these so-called Pelham Cadets—a sort of Mobile JV team comprised of boys too young for regular military service, drafted at the last minute as the true extent of the Northern threat to Mobile Bay revealed itself—Union forces moved to within 1,700 feet of the fort's walls. There, they established a siege line spanning the width of the island, deploying field guns including eight 30-pounder Parrott rifles, each weighing more than two tons.

Only six of Fort Gaines's twenty-six guns could be brought to bear on its landward side. There were as many as 864 Confederates effectively trapped inside the fort's walls, many more men than the fort was designed to comfortably hold. Reinforcement and resupply seemed unlikely.

In January 1861, Fort Gaines was finally nearing completion after decades of delay. That month, it was seized by the Alabama state militia. Construction was finished under Confederate auspices over the next year.

Fort Gaines features an earthen parapet that stands independent of its brick curtain wall. Even if this outer wall collapsed under enemy bombardment, gunners on the barbette tier could continue to fire uninterrupted. Known as a detached scarp, this design was almost unique within the Third System and reflected the latest military thinking out of France, by way of tireless innovator Joseph Totten.

Beyond the earthen embankment shielding the far side of the casemates are a series of gun ports in the curtain wall. These evenly spaced positions for small arms fire allowed the fort's garrison to mount an effective resistance against any hostile force attempting a *coup de main*—a direct assault on the fort.

A thirty-five-foot wide dry moat surrounds the curtain walls of Fort Gaines, which themselves stand a foreboding twenty-two feet tall.

The outer walls of Fort Gaines form a pentagon, each side of which originally featured ten firing positions. A bastion stands at every corner, each with embrasures for four flank howitzers. Even the fort's Union attackers would not proceed too close to the fort out of a well-placed fear that a howitzer in the opposite bastion might rake them with canister shot.

Out in the bay, the naval engagement was over, and Fort Powell, which guarded the rear approach to Fort Gaines, surrendered without a fight. The USS *Chickasaw*, one of Farragut's three surviving ironclads, turned its attention to Fort Gaines, opening fire on its vulnerable northern flank. One Rebel later explained,

> The very first shot fired ... penetrated the casemate and killed two of our sick. The magazine were no better, and had a single shell struck ... either of them the whole garrison would have been blown to kingdom come. ...We could render Mobile no assistance; we could render Morgan no assistance; and we could have done no harm to the enemy, for every gun we had that bore upon the fleet was dismounted, except the small smooth bore, at which they would have laughed in derision.

In 1864, a drawbridge spanned the dry moat at the sally port. The space beyond was occupied by various support buildings, including barracks for the fort's garrison. Upon the approach of the Union Army, the very soldiers quartered in these buildings burnt them to the ground, robbing the enemy of any cover from their defensive fire, before retreating behind the walls of Fort Gaines.

Facing west over the parade ground at Fort Gaines, starting on the left is the quartermaster's storehouse, followed by the officer's quarters. The sidewalk leads directly to the sally port. To the right of this, on the north side of the parade, are a blacksmith's shop, latrine, and bakery. On the far right is a gun emplacement added to the fort around the turn of the twentieth century.

From this vantage point atop the east bastion, the men of Fort Gaines watched in relative helplessness while Farragut's fleet successfully ran the minefield. With wooden piles driven into the already shallow western end of the channel, the Union fleet was confined to the narrow passage directly beneath Fort Morgan's guns, three miles distant.

A shell fired from the USS *Chickasaw* arched over the parade and struck the interior of the south curtain wall, leaving this crater. While the shot inflicted only superficial damage to the fort itself, it was far more devastating to morale—if a Union shell could land here, the fleet in the bay could light up Fort Gaines at will. The garrison surrendered soon after.

Recognizing their fate written on the wall in shattered brick, the beleaguered Confederate garrison petitioned their commanding officer, Colonel Charles D. Anderson, requesting that he surrender the fort in order to save their lives.

Anderson initially resisted. But another three days of sporadic bombardment ensued, pressure from within the overcrowded fort mounted, and on August 8, Anderson admitted defeat, surrendering a largely intact Fort Gaines to his Northern adversaries.

Across the pass, an outraged Confederate General Page reported to his superiors:

> Yesterday morning at daylight Colonel Anderson communicated with enemy by flag of truce without my sanction. I immediately asked him by signal purpose of it. He made no acknowledgment, though I ... telegraphed repeatedly ... "Hold on to your fort." I went there last night and was greatly surprised to find Colonel Anderson absent in the fleet, making terms for surrender. I gave peremptory orders on his return ... all terms were annulled and he was relieved from command. This morning fired signal guns and telegraphed same effect. No reply. At 9:30 o'clock enemy's flag hoisted on Fort Gaines. Colonel Anderson's conduct inexplicable and disgraceful.

Confederate President Jefferson Davis also condemned Anderson's actions. When word of Fort Gaines's surrender reached the capital at Richmond, Davis fumed, "The conduct ... seems to be discreditable to our arms. The officers responsible for the surrenders will be held to a strict account for their acts as soon as practicable."

Good thing for Coronel Anderson, then, that he would sit out the rest of the conflict in the protective custody of Union forces, a prisoner of war until the fall of the Confederacy in nine months' time.

I get their frustration; Page and Davis wanted to win. In their shoes, I would be crestfallen, too, as yet another in a long line of battles went sideways right before my eyes.

But far from inexplicable, as Page put it, or discreditable, as Davis said, I find Anderson's surrender to be maybe the most compelling act of the whole battle. I doubt it was an easy decision for him, a well-respected officer who had faithfully devoted four years of his life to the Rebel cause. Yet Anderson was able to set these passions aside. He was the only man among the three who could see the big picture with any real clarity.

Anderson's actions call to us across time, begging us to wrestle with very subjective, but nonetheless imperative questions, such as: Was the defense of Mobile Bay, against his once and future countrymen no less, not even some marauding horde from over the sea, worth a wholesale and completely senseless slaughter of the men at Fort Gaines? Was one more bloodstained spot on the map, no matter how valiantly fought, going to save the Confederacy in the latter half of 1864?

I guess the way you answer those questions depends almost entirely on how you grapple with this one: Is sending your twelve year-old son into the fray a heroic last line of defense—or the first sign that all for which you've been fighting is slipping through your fingers?

Days before, the citizens of Mobile had talked themselves into believing that it was reasonable to ask boys, young enough to be *playing* fort, to defend one in real life.

And then there's Anderson, defying an emerging Lost Cause mentality, pausing to inhale deeply, and asking: "Is victory at all costs even a victory at all?"

Here is a dizzying look down the spiral stairs inside a corner bastion. Each of the fort's five bastions were designed to be independently defensible, the scene of a bitter final resistance in the event a breach of the fort's outer defenses.

Cool sunlight filters into the bastion via the ventilation ports, a long tunnel leading to the parade, and four large embrasures, ready to accommodate 24-pounder flank howitzers. The floor of the bastion doubles as a cover plate for the cistern used to store rainwater collected on the terreplein above.

A long reinforced tunnel links each bastion to the parade. If the enemy somehow made it onto the parade, they would still have to fight their way down this claustrophobic, ricochet-prone space to subdue any defenders who chose to make a last stand inside the bastion.

Ditto for the enlisted men's latrine, designed to support a desperate last stand by any defenders who might have been answering nature's call when things outside went down the tube. The long trench below the bench seen here flushed with the tidal action of the bay, making this a fairly pleasant bathroom experience by nineteenth-century standards.

It's not clear that the officer's latrine could withstand the same onslaught as its enlisted counterpart. Located on the opposite side of the parade, behind the officer's quarters, it certainly would have been more private, though.

The south gun ramp once allowed soldiers to push heavy ammunition carts between magazines on the parade level and firing positions on the upper terreplein with relative ease.

Thirty-two-pounder cannons once occupied these positions behind the brick parapet on the Fort Gaines's south flank. In the modern day, their field of fire is obscured by a stand of trees, but this space would have been actively cleared during the fort's heyday, allowing crews to target any hostile ships in the Gulf of Mexico.

5

THE ENDICOTT PERIOD BATTERIES

Battery Stanton is a reinforced concrete Endicott Period coastal gun battery built on historic Fort Gaines. Construction began in 1899. The battery was activated in May 1901. It originally consisted of two 6-inch M1897MI rifles. A third emplacement, mounting a 6-inch M1903, was added between 1903 and 1904.

As well-maintained public parks, Forts Morgan and Gaines have been infiltrated by anachronisms—intruders from later periods, trespassing upon the strata of an earlier one. To the keen-eyed visitor, the whole tableau is like some kind of *Highlights* magazine spread in which the game is to spot wacky items that don't belong to the Third System.

For example, you'll find handrails where none existed in the nineteenth century, a concession to the fine print of some modern insurance policy. Detailed informational plaques abound—a few of the historical quotes featured in this book came to my attention on these sun-worn tablets of ancient wisdom. There are occasional lampposts and light fixtures, too, which would have mystified Yankee and Rebel alike. Had such lights existed in their day, they'd have served as homing beacons for enemy guns. These civilian conveniences are the accoutrement of a decades-long afterlife as open-air museums dedicated to the Third System.

But the most obvious modifications at Forts Morgan and Gaines fall into yet another category. They are military upgrades which enabled the forts to carry on their coastal defense mission for a full eighty years after their Civil War heyday. They manifest around Forts Morgan and Gaines as grim concrete and iron hulks grafted atop the older brick casemates, which end up looking almost dainty by comparison.

These are the Endicott Period batteries, dating from 1895-1910—an era in which the United States military began to employ such cutting-edge technologies as electricity, breech-loading rifled artillery, disappearing gun carriages, concrete, and rebar.

How did coastal defense evolve into this—a form wholly unconcerned with curtain walls, bastions, or sally ports?

During the Civil War, the Union leveraged its modern warships—propelled by steam, clad in iron, and sporting rifled artillery—to great effect against Confederate-held Third System fortifications. Plus or minus a pithy catchphrase, Farragut's handy capture of Mobile Bay was pretty typical of these confrontations—whether or not a brick and mortar fort posed any serious impediment to this new generation of battleships was very much an open question.

The masonry forts of the Third System were not immediately abandoned, however. Most, including Forts Morgan and Gaines, were restored to battle-readiness even before the end of the Civil War.

Battery Stanton was two stories tall, with guns mounted on the second level and magazines on the first, sheltered underneath a reinforced concrete ceiling. The battery occupied most of the eastern two walls of Fort Gaines.

But by the 1870s, many of these aging behemoths were falling one by one into disrepair. The nation's military attentions had turned to the subjugation of native peoples in the west. The public had little appetite for foreign war—and few obvious enemies abroad in any event—so budgets for coastal defense began to shrink.

This giant slab separated the two original batteries, shielding one in the event that the other was struck by enemy fire. It also offers a pretty vivid measure of just how imposing the hulk of an Endicott Period battery could be.

This track was a part of a hoisting system that allowed crews to move the M1897MI's 108-pound shells out of the magazine with relative safety and ease using a sling. Each shell was hurled aloft on nearly 30 lbs. of powder and had a maximum effective range of 14,509 yards.

The east bastion of Fort Gaines was filled during the construction of Battery Stanton. In the modern day, a visitor can just barely crawl inside—if they don't mind sandy knees or the idea of the lumbering weight which hangs ominously overhead.

The M1903 rifle on Battery One was redeployed to France during World War I. The two M1897MI rifles at Batteries Two and Three were scrapped when Battery Stanton was finally deactivated in 1932. Still present are the iron treads of the stairwells, rusted but intact—not as flashy as the big guns, perhaps, but a relatively rare sight among Endicott Period batteries in the Southeast.

Battery Stanton was equipped with several davits, small cranes for hoisting shells from the parade level to the firing level.

This artillery spotter position was equipped with these simple but effective "sound tubes," which amplified the spotter's voice based on the same principles at work when one creates a cone in front of one's mouth with one's hands.

Battery Stanton was powered by a 20KW steam driven electric plant, upgraded in 1921 to a 25KW generator running on gasoline. Both power plants were sheltered under reinforced concrete in the cavernous rooms below the guns. Today, the caretakers have converted this into a fine museum space showcasing the history of the fort.

The magazine on the southeast corner of the parade highlights the robust construction typical of coastal defense in the Endicott Period. These walls are easily two feet thick and encased in a similar amount of earth—a cross section that helps one to visualize the devastating potential of the cutting-edge artillery deployed by the world's great navies at the turn of the twentieth century.

The Third System quartermaster's office sits directly beneath Battery Stanton. The southeast corner of the structure was even lopped off to accommodate the massive footprint of the later structure.

All three guns at Battery Stanton rested on disappearing carriages. Crews serviced and loaded guns while in a resting position below the parapet; the carriages could rapidly raise the gun over the parapet to fire before quickly disappearing again, like a gopher into a hole. Both crews and guns—with their massive barrels, more than 23 feet long—were safer from enemy fire under this configuration.

Battery Terrett (1901-1923) sits just outside the northeast flank of Fort Gaines. It consisted of three 3-inch M1898MI rapid fire guns mounted on M1898 masking parapets. These lightweight guns were meant to harass any enemy minesweepers set upon the Endicott-era minefield that had replaced its primitive Confederate predecessor.

Power was supplied by the generator at Battery Stanton. Endicott batteries featured no fortifications against ground attack or siege. During an era in which naval power was presumed to be the true measure of a nation's military might, faith was placed in big guns, minefields, and other measures that deterred an enemy from landing in the first place.

In 1885, President Grover Cleveland appointed a joint Army, Navy, and civilian board, headed by Secretary of War William Endicott, and tasked them with reviewing the status of America's coastal defenses after this long fallow period. Like the earlier Third System committee, they returned a sobering report, confirming that the nation's coastal defenses were indeed outmoded and neglected. More noteworthy was their recommendation for $127 million worth of new, cutting edge fortifications at some twenty-nine locations along the nation's coasts, including Mobile.

The Endicott Board of Fortifications described the persistent vulnerabilities of Mobile Bay—the same weaknesses which Farragut's fleet had exploited twenty years earlier:

> Mobile has a large shipping trade in cotton and lumber. Population, 29,132. Nineteen and a half feet can be carried over bar at entrance of bay, and 18 feet can be carried through dredged channel 21 miles long to city. The city is 30 miles from outer bar. In case of an enemy's vessel attempting to enter, the dredged channel could be closed and none but very light-draught vessels could approach close enough to the city to shell it. Vessels drawing less than 16 feet could with safety approach within 4 miles of the city, and could shell it from any position on bay to southward.

Across the channel, Fort Morgan received a huge new cantonment—hundreds of soldiers across three companies of Coastal Artillery, manning five batteries, occupying 100 support buildings ranging from barracks, officer housing, a bakery, a gymnasium, a power and ice plant, morgue, and a darkroom. Young women were even ferried from Mobile to this otherwise fully functioning town for regularly scheduled dances.

The engineer's wharf allowed for emergency deployment of the updated minefield—a cornerstone of harbor defense during the Endicott Period—as well as easy delivery of ordinance and other supplies to the batteries at Fort Morgan. Today, the crumbled pilings have been left to the wading birds—in this case, a great blue heron casting about for breakfast.

Construction on Battery Bowyer began in 1897. This massive structure, powered by its own 5-KW generator, was armed with four 8-inch guns mounted on disappearing carriages. Battery Bowyer is structurally unsound in the modern day and is cordoned off to the public for this reason.

In late 1917, at the height of World War I, the four guns of Battery Bowyer were removed and allocated for redeployment to other theaters. Located at the heart of the bustling cantonment, the battery did not languish for long—by 1920, rooms in the concrete belly of the beast were occupied by telephone switchboards and a radio station.

During periods when the post was on a low level of alert, powder was stored here, in the 1,462-square-foot peace magazine, located a safe distance away from the base's batteries and living quarters.

It wasn't some accident that blew sky high the roof of the peace magazine. The men stationed at Fort Morgan had a perfect safety record on this count. Rather, this sunny makeover was the work of Hurricane Frederick in 1979.

Battery Dearborn, named for Thomas Jefferson's Secretary of War, was active between 1901 and 1931. It mounted eight 12-inch M1890MI mortars arranged in groups of four across two mortar pits, designated A and B. Each 13-ton monster fired 824-pound shells to a maximum range of seven miles.

Fire control was supplied via telephone and wooden signboard from this signaling station. A team of thirty-one men was assigned to each mortar: twelve men for firing, nineteen for moving shells and powder from the magazine.

The mount for a long-removed generator still adorns one of the darkened rooms inside Battery Dearborn. This once must have been a loud and bilious assignment for the men who tended it—exponentially so when the massive mortars next door were fired.

Of particular concern to the Endicott Board were those shallow draught vessels. Tall wooden ships of earlier generations rode low in the water, but the ironclad monitors of Farragut's fleet had drawn only 13.5 feet. These more modern ships could move beyond the dredged channel, menacing Mobile and all commerce coming and going from that city—and there wasn't a thing that the slow-firing, muzzle loading guns still mounted at Forts Morgan and Gaines could do about it.

To address these vulnerabilities, the Endicott Board recommended that Mobile receive twelve 12-inch breech loading rifled guns weighing 50 tons apiece, capable of targeting enemy ships at a distance; ten 8-inch breech loading rifled guns, each weighing 13 tons, to harass minesweepers or other enemy ships in the channel; and sixteen 12-inch rifled mortars to shell from above the lightly-armored decks of enemy ships. Though other ports were scheduled to receive torpedo boats, the board concluded that the three-mile pass between Forts Morgan and Gaines could be adequately defended by these guns, augmented with a new remote controlled minefield, to be rapidly deployed upon threat of hostilities.

The Endicott Period batteries—supplemented with later Taft Board, World War I, and World War II-era upgrades across four decades—would ultimately deploy hundreds of large caliber, long-range guns along America's coastlines. Maintaining this constant state of defensive readiness was a truly Sisyphean effort, as each innovation in defense would invariably be outclassed in short order by some advance in an enemy's offensive capabilities. For example, some Endicott emplacements in use during World War II were compelled to reckon with threats like strafing and aerial bombing—techniques made possible by technologies inconceivable to the Endicott Board.

Like the Third System before it, however, the Endicott batteries as a whole saw direct engagement against foreign aggressors at a vanishingly low rate. The seven coastal batteries at Mobile Bay, in use between 1899 and 1945, never had occasion to fire upon an enemy vessel.

Battery Dearborn is almost completely overrun by brush, easily one of the most striking sights at modern Fort Morgan.

Aging cisterns dot the landscape, a rain collection scheme hatched to supply fresh water for the hundreds of men once stationed on this narrow peninsula.

Battery Duportail (1900-1931), viewed from inside a casemate, was built on the south end of Fort Morgan's parade, where it partially obscures the footprint of the old citadel. This battery was named after Major General Louis L. Duportail, Chief of Engineers to the Continental Army from 1777 to 1783, the first in a line of Frenchmen to occupy similar roles during the U.S.'s early decades.

Operating the two guns at Battery Duportail required a team of eighty-five men working in concert with another team of eighteen specialists—range officers, observers, and plotters who tracked the fall of Duportail's shot, estimated the distance of an enemy's ship, and calculated adjustments to the gun's angle of fire accordingly.

Like the rest of the Endicott batteries at Mobile Bay, the powerful guns at Battery Duportail never saw combat. But unlike the sleepy, halcyon days at Fort Morgan described by William T. Sherman, crews in this period trained with great discipline most every day, remaining in a constant state of readiness for an attack that never came.

Battery Duportail mounted two 12-inch M1888MII guns on M1896 disappearing gun carriages. The M1888MII could hurl a 1,040-pound shell—available in several flavors, such as armor piercing and high explosive—up to eight-and-a-half miles.

Duportail is a two-story battery with space below for magazines, a 30-KW generator, and intel rooms where the specialists worked. The generator powered lighting, mechanical shell hoists, and motors for retracting the disappearing gun carriages on the emplacements overhead.

A striking contrast—spindly, spider-like columns of reinforced concrete replaced the arched brick casemates of Fort Morgan, which can be seen in all their monumental bulk just across the parade.

These handprints were made by more recent explorers, but many individuals have left their mark on these fortifications over the years. During its prime, the base was home to many officers' families, including children, and at least a few long-term relationships blossomed out of the post dances.

A turntable for the Endicott Period rail system, almost certainly rusted into place, remains on the parade in front of Battery Duportail.

An advocate for national defense would argue that *not* using a coastal battery is perhaps the strongest possible indicator of its efficacy. A good return on investment, it has deterred any foreign threat so thoroughly as to render the very notion of an assault on the United States unthinkable. Since the advent of the Third System, the United States has rarely spared any expense in the realm of the national defense. And as reward for those efforts, the nation hasn't fought a foreign adversary along its continental coastline since the War of 1812. The world recognizes our power and wisely steers clear—or so one version of the logic goes.

On one hand, we should be careful not to attribute U.S. security *solely* to the size and number of our guns. What about our diplomatic efforts, the goodwill borne of trade, the projection of our naval power globally, international factors far beyond our control, and so on? And yet, it's hard to deny: when the nation and its people are convinced that something is important, the expansive financial and technical resources brought to bear on that problem are truly remarkable.

An afternoon at Fort Morgan or Fort Gaines, taking in more than a century of defensive measures ranging from Third System counterscarps to Endicott Period mortar pits, should convince you of that.

The men tasked with defending our shores didn't take the challenge before them lightly. Living in the generally free and largely functioning society that we've inherited, I'm certainly thankful for their caretaking efforts, whatever exact share of the credit they deserve.

The Endicott Period barracks were two-story wooden structures with plentiful windows and broad, airy porches built to catch the cooling breeze. Today, all that remains of these palaces for the rank and file of the Coast Artillery Corps are their foundations— askew in the soft sand like the teeth of a doddering old man.

Built between March and May of 1898, Battery Thomas was the first Endicott Period emplacement at Mobile Bay, rushed into service as the nation revved its war machine in advance of the Spanish-American War. Towering high over Fort Morgan's counterscarp, it is also one of the most visually arresting structures at Mobile Point.

Its dizzying stature was also its undoing. A 1915 study concluded that Battery Thomas's remarkable height made it extremely vulnerable to enemy bombardment. It would be deactivated in 1917.

Battery Thomas shows its age. Constructed directly on top of a huge mound of sand, it has fractured in ways that its more stable, younger siblings have not.

Battery Thomas mounted two 4.72-inch rapid fire Armstrong rifles, weapons of British design and manufacture. These weapons would be abandoned for American-made guns as the Endicott Period progressed. The battery was to harass enemy minesweepers attempting to dismantle the minefield, which would have been deployed just offshore from Battery Thomas.

The battery had no generator of its own and instead drew its electricity from the power plant located inside the walls of old Fort Morgan at Battery Duportail.

In 1919, the decommissioned battery was converted into a range-finding station for its sister and ultimate successor, Battery Schenck, which was constructed right next door, with a lower, less vulnerable profile and the same mission as the defunct Battery Thomas.

The base at Fort Morgan was deactivated in 1931 and turned over to the state of Alabama. In this period, the first steps were taken to turn the formerly strategic Mobile Point into a state park.

The draw then wasn't much different than it is today: come and play fort! As the newly dedicated park found its footing at the height of the Great Depression, there were still several coastal defense guns rusting in place, as well as an entire freshly-abandoned military cantonment to explore.

Battery Schenck (1900-1923) mounted two 3-inch M1898MI guns plus one 3-inch M1902 added in 1904. Like most Endicott batteries, Schenck was named for a fallen U.S. serviceman—in this case, 1st Lt. William T. Schenck, 25th U.S. Infantry, who was killed in action against insurgent Filipinos during the Philippine-American War (1899-1902). Today, you can buy a Coke in its shade.

In April 1942, Fort Morgan was reactivated. Elements of Battery F and G, 50th U.S. Coast Artillery Corps were deployed to Mobile Point and equipped with four 155mm M1918M1 guns on modern Panama mounts. Comprised of approximately 200 men, this position was christened Battery 155, the Temporary Harbor Defense of Mobile, which lasted until July 1944.

6

WE ARE LOSING THE NEXT WAR FOR COASTAL DEFENSE

These days, the cracked bricks of Fort Morgan and Fort Gaines, fired to withstand the fury of war, are more likely bring to mind an elegant turn-of-the-twentieth-century garden walk or some mothballed industrial plant from several lifetimes ago.

The guns that once bristled like so many vicious thorns over the parapets have long since fallen silent. Many of them were melted down as scrap or redeployed to European battlefields at moments of great crisis during the last century—at the onset of World War I, for example, their historical value equal to exactly zilch before the looming threat of war.

In the twenty-first century, it isn't the Spanish, the British, or the Germans who menace these shores. This is no Civil War, either. The integrity of Alabama is under threat from a changing climate. And once again, the coastal defenses of Mobile Bay are on the front line.

According to the National Oceanic and Atmospheric Administration, global mean sea level rose approximately nine inches between 1880 and 2018, with the period after 1993 accounting for more than a third of the total increase. Conservative predictions by the same agency put the increase over the next century at more than a foot, with worst case scenarios projected at over eight feet—meaning that even under modest scenarios, Forts Morgan (approximately six feet above sea level) and Gaines (four feet) will be impacted dramatically, perhaps catastrophically.

Already, water levels in the ditch at Fort Morgan, especially at high tide, are regulated by a pumping system housed in a nondescript building near Battery Thomas. Like surface-to-air missiles or drones, this is a problem of which neither the Third System commission nor the Endicott Board could ever have dreamed.

Poor drainage from Fort Morgan's terreplein has been an issue since the 1830s. Intrusion from this source has destabilized the casemates, threatening the long-term integrity of the fort itself. An extensive preservation program is ongoing, but increased

The pump house, seen here dwarfed by the counterscarp of Fort Morgan and the towering Battery Thomas, helps to confine encroaching water to the cunette , maintaining a dry moat, rather than a wet one.

Remnants of the Endicott Period post can be found all over the park surrounding Fort Morgan. Rising seas threaten to inundate the pine forest that has overtaken the old cantonment, reducing Mobile Point to little more than a shifting spit of sand.

flooding will undermine these efforts. It isn't science fiction to say that before the end of the twenty-first century, the parade could become a fulltime swamp in the middle of a collapsing fort.

Across the pass, a retention wall barely two dozen feet from Fort Gaines is a popular fishing destination. While scenic, this proximity to the Gulf of Mexico now imperils the fort's very existence. Already, a pump purges water out of the southwest bastion, depositing it in the low-lying moat that girds the two landward sides of the fort. Seawater inundated these forts in 2005 when Katrina hit. In 2020, Hurricane Sally put both forts underwater again, this time adding heavier rain to mix. Such hurricanes are only increasing in intensity and unpredictability as our climate continues to warm.

Imagine what would happen if such a storm made landfall, stalling over Dauphin Island and Mobile Point the way Hurricane Dorian parked over the Bahamas in 2019? Even setting aside the potential loss of human life, that's a grim scenario that could seal the fate of our beloved historic forts.

If you're skeptical, a quick internet search for images of Louisiana's Third System defenses offers a glimpse of a not-too-far-fetched future already come to pass. Go look it up.

Fort Morgan's sieve-like terreplein is now the least of its issues with water. Sea level rise could saturate the ground beneath the fort's foundations, destabilizing the entire structure. Many forts in the Third System face a similar hazard.

Vegetation has taken hold on the face of Fort Morgan. The tiny roots of these humble weeds are capable of prying apart this bomb-resistant masonry arch in the slowest of motion.

At Fort Morgan, lime and calcium leach from bricks and the mortar in between, forming substantial surface deposits, a natural occurrence in the humid coastal air, but also a sure sign of water intrusion from above.

A United States Geodetic Survey maker is located on the barbette tier of Fort Gaines, seemingly as rock solid and permanent a landmark as anything man might make. In 2011, Fort Gaines was listed by National Trust for Historic Preservation as one of America's Eleven Most Endangered Historic Places.

Meanwhile, our politicians quibble disingenuously about the exact causes, even as our scientists and soldiers harmonize to action.

Since 2010, the Pentagon has included climate change as a significant factor in its National Defense Strategy review. This is a modern-day iteration of the Endicott Board, a report issued every four years assessing national defense strategy and readiness. Their conclusion has been consistent—that climate change presents a very real threat to the nation, requiring specific strategic responses.

Our best military minds recognize that simply hardening the target isn't going to work this time—that perhaps the best way to protect our corner of the Earth is to tread more lightly upon it. These hardboiled warriors are beginning to talk like hippies—less about thicker walls and instead about clean energy and sustainability.

In this century, Forts Morgan and Gaines themselves retain no strategic importance. All the same, the defensive line staked out by these impressive forts should not be yielded.

There are some who say climate change is a long-term collective action problem, one which we as a species are poorly evolved to address. We are short-term thinkers, they opine. We're simply not very good at thinking so far ahead or in such abstract

It seems as if a structure like this was built to last forever. After almost two centuries, Fort Morgan's sally port still cuts an impressive figure—but the Alabama Historical Commission, now in charge of the site, will struggle to protect it from the worst effects of a rising sea.

The neglected upper level of Battery Dearborn, thoroughly reclaimed by coastal scrub, carries its own warning label: "Danger. Explore at your own risk." Challenge accepted.

Fort Gaines is at the center of a well-used green space administered by the Dauphin Island Park and Beach Board.

The silent guns at Forts Morgan and Gaines come to life during regularly scheduled historical reenactments at both forts, the perfect opportunity to get a taste of how these spaces must have bustled during their nineteenth-century heyday.

terms. The immediate benefits of doing nothing, of continuing our carefree business as usual, loom far greater in our lizard brains than the abstract consequences, which will be suffered most seriously decades down the line—not by us, but by our kids.

That line of argument does not sound too different from one advanced in the waning, increasingly hopeless days of the Confederacy, when a unit of untested teenagers were tasked with the defense of Mobile. A last ditch, worry-about-the-problem-when-it's-too-late kind of measure—it's certainly not the line of thinking that resulted in the preemptive construction of the Third System of coastal fortifications. And that may be the most profound historical lesson on display at Forts Morgan and Gaines.

As a people, we have risen to meet threats far more abstract and remote than climate change—like hypothetical invasions from mostly-disinterested European powers based a hemisphere away. Are these forts, physical testament to the foresight and sacrifice of earlier generations of Americans, fated to bear silent witness as that for which our forebears fought sinks beneath the waves?

Losing the war for our coastlines to the very sea itself seems like the most unpatriotic course of all.

The homes and vacation rentals of Mobile Bay stand tall on stilts of wood—a precaution against the devastating surge and furious waves suffered in previous hurricanes. We rest our heads easily on beautiful evenings like these, when trouble seems so far away.

The sun sets on the Gulf Coast of Alabama, as it always has. How much ground will be yielded before it rises again?